HOW TO FRANCHISE YOUR OWN BUSINESS
OBTAIN FINANCIAL FREEDOM
AND
INCREASE YOUR WEALTH ALONG THE WAY

VIN LAURENTE

"Unless the Lord builds the house, the builders labor in vain"
Psalm 127:1 (New International Version)

The nature of the franchise business in not that complicated. It adheres to the same set of business principles employed by all businessmen. It may have some variations but still the business fundamentals are similar.

When starting your own franchise business, it is imperative that the important aspects will be processed and not a single stone will be left unturned.

How to Franchise Your Own Business
Obtain Financial Freedom and Increase Your Wealth Along the Way
Copyright 2022@Vin Laurente

Published by: Magn8 Ventures Inc.
ISBN 978-621-96233-3-9 (Paperback Edition)

INTRODUCTION

Imagine this. You started one store and in a very short span of time, it became very successful. The revenue is soaring and so massive that the customers kept coming to your store in unprecedented numbers. You also received multiple inquiries from people from walks of life if you are planning to expand in other locations all across the country.

This enormous positive feedback encouraged you to have this audacity to dream higher and bigger and decided to up the ante of the game.

You draw up a business plan and based on your forecast, you can easily multiply your stores in multiple locations bringing much revenue to sustain chain operations.

The business plan also suggests that the financial and non-financial data all sum up to one thing, you can duplicate the success of your stores even in other locations using the same formula that you implemented in your current store. Your store will also be an instant crowd drawer given the quality and price of your products and the services that you offer.

Faced with this bright reality, you are now confronted with two choices, one is to expand your store operations by utilizing the financial resources in your hands and the other one is to expand your store chain operations using the financial resources of would be partners and investors, what would you do?

Normally, if you are very conservative, you will take the traditional way and slowly expand your business using your own resources. It's normal human instinct. The drawback of this is, over time, your financial strength would be stretched out and it will not suffice the growing demands of your chain operations. Also, the manpower requirements will be limited to your family members and most likely your most trusted circle friends. You can expand but only up to certain number of stores. There will be limitations for this kind of set-up.

For those who are risk takers, they will take the road less travelled and jumped on the bandwagon and go into franchising. They see gargantuan opportunities by venturing into uncharted territories. The pot of gold is shining at the end of the rainbow.

What is a franchise? According to Merriam Webster dictionary, " it is the right or license granted to an individual or group to market a company's goods or services in a particular territory."

What will drive a particular business owner to go into franchising? He may have considered the various tangibles and intangibles such as access to more capital, access to the best talent, expansion of his business will be a lot faster and the brand will become valuable in the near future. He might also consider entering a whole new world where everything and anything is possible.

Another prime consideration is it is every man's dream to augment his income by venturing into a business that will not only satisfy not only their own needs but will also have an immediate impact on their immediate family members who rely on them for financial security.

All over the world, based on the current statistics which are readily available on the internet, the demand for franchise business is increasing at a very fast and magnificent pace driven by the goal of every businessman and franchisor to expand their businesses and increase their income by sharing to other people who are financially-ready their newfound financial success.

Franchising is the way for would be franchisee who want to get into the track by venturing into a business which has a proven track record of operational and financial success.

Over the years, I have seen hundreds of different businesses which flourished by boldly taking the franchising route. They became the engine of growth of majority of the countries all over the world from the United States, Canada, Europe, Asia and in almost all countries where franchising is present.

In Asia alone, the Philippines is the most aggressive when it comes to franchising. Considering that almost 95% of the businesses in this country is composed of the Micro Small and Medium Enterprises (MSMEs), it's not surprising that it became an instant phenomenon with more and more companies pivoting their business model to shift to franchising .

Combined with the innate creativity and highest literacy rate in the country, the Philippines is the trailblazer in all things about franchising.

With the advent of the internet, the world becomes a smaller place and almost everyone can easily talk to each other even though they came from two distant locations. The internet is the greatest creations of all times for everyone can get instant access to unlimited information about business ideas and others.

Cross promotions and marketing of franchise business can also be done in mixed channels such as You Tube, Facebook and Linked in.

Franchising has really entered a very exciting era where the fusion of old school ideas and modern technology will make wonders and push the business into its maximum potential.

I wrote this book for simple reason that I want to share to everyone the humble ideas that I believe will give you guidance if you are planning to take the plunge and go into franchising. These are practical tips that you can apply in your daily lives.

" When I saw (Maurice and Richard McDonald's restaurant in San Bernardino, California), working that day in 1954, I felt like some latter-day Newton who'd just had an Idaho potato caromed off his skull. That night in my motel room, I did a lot of heavy thinking about what I'd seen during

that day. Visions of McDonald's restaurants dotting crossroads all over the country paraded through my brain."

Ray Kroc-American entrepreneur best known for expanding McDonald's from a local chain to the world's most profitable restaurant

OVERVIEW OF FRANCHISING

Franchising started way back in the Middle ages and over the years transformed itself into a more formal set-up.

The modern franchising started when the Singer Company implemented a franchising plan in the 1850s to distribute its sewing machines. Since then, string of companies adopted the system which proved to be effective and made their business profitable. Some of the famous names are McDonald, Kentucky Fried Chicken, 7-11 to a name a few.

The success of franchising in the United States encourage more and more countries to adopt the same business strategies. They patterned their ideas from this country and the foreign companies benchmarked with the pioneers and tried to improve and adopt the same methods that will fit their systems. The franchise industry is very peculiar in every country and franchisors must always consider the language and cultural considerations, economic conditions, government policies and technology aspects.

Franchising is such a lovely and magical word. It is very enticing as well. Imagine, if you have an existing business and you wanted to expand, one of best ways to do it is to go into franchising.

The basic idea of franchising is to start three to five company owned stores. This is to give the owner the feel of operating multiple stores or outlets. By then, he or she will be able to form and devise a system that will be the basis for chain operations management. It is important that this matter will be done so as to enable the franchisor to make adjustment and fine tuning if ever he or she decides to embark on franchising.

According to Wikipedia, " supply chain management (SCM) is the management of flow of goods and services which includes all processes that transform raw materials into final products between businesses and locations. This can include the movement and storage of raw materials, work-in-process inventory, finished goods and end to end order fulfillment from the point of origin to the point of consumption. Interconnected, interrelated or interlinked networks, channels and node businesses combine in the provision of products and services required by end customers in supply chain".

Once an individual goes into franchising, this will be the trend, franchisees will ask for guidance in running his or her store and how can a franchisor impart his or her knowledge if he or she doesn't have the first hand experience in running his or her personal store.

Knowledge of chain operations management will be the critical factor in running a very successful franchise operations particularly for franchisors.

Without it, the operations of the franchise system as whole will be compromised.

" Employ your time in improving yourself by other men's writings, so that you shall gain easily what others have labored hard for."

Socrates, Greek philosopher

CHAPTER 1

EDUCATION IS THE KEY TO SUCCESS

Education whether it is a formal one or an acquired knowledge is a big contributory factor on how we are going to become very rich and successful. There may be some persons who became very rich although they did not finish their formal education but there will come a time that you will realize how valuable education will be. This is a wealth that cannot be stolen.

There is a very big advantage if an individual has a very strong educational foundation. You can also learn though observation, by reading newspapers and magazines, browsing and reading internet resource materials among others. The internet is the greatest invention of all times. Today, all people with access to the internet can read almost everything about all topics whether it is finance, entrepreneurship, business, taxation and motivational topics. That's the beauty of it. The playing field is now equal and everyone has the same opportunity to participate in the discussion whether they are residing in a small or big countries. Even the remotest area of the earth has now internet access, thanks to the Starlink satellite internet of Elon Musk.

Make it a habit to read successful and inspirational books written by greatest authors. Let us fill our minds with positive and motivational ideas for us to grow and become rich. Spend your money on books, which are considered investments rather than expense.

Here are some of the books that I recommend for your reading:

How I Raised Myself from Failure to Success in Selling by Frank Bettger

Think and Grow Rich by Napoleon Hill

You Can Work Your Own Miracles by Napoleon Hill

Born to Win by Zig Ziglar

Art of War by Sun Tzu

When I was young, my parents used to tell us that success in life will begin once I finish my studies. That's why I valued education so much. We don't have electricity back then. All we are using was a kerosone lamp. We don't even have a television set. My father is a farmer and my mother is a simple housewife who cooked ricecakes (bibingka) for us to survive and get through life.

I remember back then that I had to wake up very early, sometimes 3 o'clock in the morning to accompany my mother who is preparing to cook ricecakes. While I am conversing with her, I am reviewing for my exam. This is our bonding moments. In between, my mother will tell stories how they grew up, how challenging it is to be born in poor family and how she wanted to finish high school but my grandmother prevented her from pursuing it because of the financial hardships during that time. My mother used to tell me, " my son, you have to finish school because that is the only inheritance that we can give to you." Those are the words that pierced through my heart. In addition to that, my grandmother on my father's side, served as the storyteller of the family. I remember it vividly that every 6 o'clock in the evening, my siblings along with my cousins, will gather together in one roof to hear her wonderful stories. The stories that I heard from my grandmother served as my model in writing this book.

Let us not waste the opportunity to improve our lives. Let us give priority to reading and education. Due to the fast paced environment brought about by the advent of modern technology, we should always study and learn the new tricks of the trade, otherwise, we will be left behind.

Many people say that there are many people who never finished their studies yet they became very successful. All I can say is that they are rare exceptions.

Everyday life is like a business. There is always one aspect of business which is involve such as budgeting, accounting, business planning and organization behavior.

Starting a business is like weaving one beautiful movie. The first thing that you will need is one good idea. An idea that will create a spark that will fit your personality as a business person. If you are fond of food, then venture into food business. If you love to write, then go on and publish your own book. If you are into technology, go and develop an app or something. There are so many aspects of business where we can go into franchising. Almost all aspects of business are franchiseable.

If you have don't have formal training and business, you can always read and research. The internet is a great equalizer. The business information can be found left and right. Grab the opportunity to learn online. It is a small world after all. You can also read the latest blogs about business here and abroad. You can always combine those ideas and make it your own. Business ideas can move and inspire people. There are so many business books that are available online. All we need is to allot time to read at least one or two hours a day. That will make all the difference between winning and losing.

" A positive mind finds a way it can be done; A negative mind looks for all the ways it can't be done"

Napoleon Hill

CHAPTER 2

POSITIVE MENTAL ATTITUDE

When I was still working with one insurance company here in the Philippines as a member of their sales team, the first thing that they thought us was to always maintain a positive mental attitude (PMA). According to our trainor, everything starts from the mind. Whatever we think, that will manifest in our lives. If you want to become rich, you will become rich. If you think you will be poor forever, most likely that will happen to you. That is why it is very important that each day when we wake up in the morning, we should start the day with PMA.

Carpe diem, quam minimum credula postero, " Seize the day, put very little trust in tomorrow (the future), that's what Roman poet Horace said.

Set aside your problems, whether it is personal or

financial, and face the day with a positive mindset.

The problem will become a greater problem if you will be problematic about it. Focus on finding solutions. The positives must always offset the negatives. Most of the times our problems are blessings in disguise and they show us the proper perspectives in life. It's how you see problems. Problems are spices of life. The challenges that we hurdle give colors in our dull life.

" I always did something I was a little not ready to do. I think that's how you grow. When there's that moment of 'Wow, I'm not really sure I can do this,' and you push through those moments, that's when you have a breakthrough."

Marissa Mayer, Yahoo CEO

CHAPTER 3

VALUABLE FRANCHISING TIPS

1 **Make a Business Plan.** Sometimes in order to succeed in life and also in business, it is imperative that we will have an idea of what we wanted to do and what we wanted to achieve before worrying about the details. Try this. Visualize your successful franchising chain (let's say 3 to 5 stores operating simultaneously). That is your target. Then from there, work out the details backwards, budget, franchising plans and others. Most of the time it works and it will help you a lot in setting your achievable goal.

Make a business plan. Benjamin Franklin once said, " By failing to plan, you are preparing to fail.". A good business plan will be your guide in operating your franchise business or any other form of business to make it successful and avoid any pitfalls that come along the way.

These are the normal contents of a business plan:

1) Executive Summary

2) Table of Contents

3) Brief Description and History of your Business (sometimes called business profile)

4) Mission and Vision

5) Description of products and services being offered

6) SWOT Analysis (Strength, Weaknesses, Opportunities and Threats)

7) Market Overview

8) Competitive Analysis

9) Marketing Strategies

10) Production or Manufacturing Plans

11) Forecasted Financial Statements (Sales and Operating Expenses in particular)

12) Contingency or exit plans

13) Other important matters that might affect the business as a whole

The business plan can be adjusted from time to time. It is merely a guide and can be altered as the business moves and grows. It is not one size fits all document. It is adjustable and the new ideas that comes along must be integrated on the original business plan.

Lean and Mean Strategy

2 Size is power but it does not necessarily mean that those who have bigger organization will become successful. Sometimes the ones having lesser personnel but with good strategies and tactics are going

to win in terms of cost benefits.

That's why guerrilla marketing is so popular nowadays because of the techniques it is employing to beat bigger guys in the market. When an organization with lesser personnel moves in the market, it can move swiftly because it will not worry about abundant costs in promoting and operating the business.

Keep only key personnel in operating your business. You will save on payroll costs too.

3 Hire the right people the first time around

If you are going to hire people for your organization, hire the right individuals the first time around. Remember that constant personnel turnover is not good for any business. It will have an overall impact in your professional bearing in the industry. Hire the best, the most honest, the most dependable and above all the right people. That's it. No ifs, no buts.

The main asset of the business aside from money is the people that it keeps. It is considered as a human capital. Invest on people because they will be the ones to make your business grow. Once your company expands, you will always need people who will oversee the operations, finance, marketing, production and promotions. It is very important that they will be able to deliver and give their best shot on the said aspects of business.

4 Benchmarking with the Pioneer

The first company in the market can teach us plenty of lessons. If you are in the food business, gather information about the best practices of the industry leaders. It can help you a lot in professionalizing the operations of your business. In times of uncertainties, the beacon of light emanates from the first one who ventured on that particular market segment. These companies mastered all the moves that keep them afloat for a longer period of time. Remember that experience is still the best teacher.

It is always very challenging to start your company from scratch. Trial and error method is always very expensive because if you miss, there will be costs involve. It is very important that you will pattern your franchise business based on the successful operations of existing franchise business.

5 Alliances and Partnerships

There is power in numbers as the most famous saying goes. If you are operating a small and medium enterprises, it's better and helpful to align and partner with associations who can help you in promoting your business and guiding you in turning it around. The intricacies of business can be easily understood with the help of professional contacts and industry friends.

In every country, there is a franchise associations

which can give you guidance if you are planning to go into franchising. You can easily look at the internet and probably ask you closest friends who are already operating a franchise business. They can help you a lot with this particular angle.

6 Savings is the Key

Cash is still King. It is important that you will monitor every aspects of your operations. You can keep track of everything by creating a daily , weekly, monthly, quarterly and annual matrix that will determine whether you are overspending in some aspects of your operations. Financial dexterity is important. If you can save, then save. When the economy is down and everything is not coming your way, Cash is still king.

If you have too much cash in your company coffers, you should find a way to re-invest it to improve the over-all operations of your company.

"Do what you love and the money will   follow."

Marsha Sinetar

CHAPTER 4

STEERING YOUR FRANCHISE BUSINESS TO SAFEST HARBOR

A business built on solid ground will withstand the tests of time. A business erected on solid foundation will flourish and will stand shoulder to shoulder and head to head with competitions.

The nature of the franchise business in not that complicated than what it seems. It adheres to the same set of business principles employed by all businessmen. It may have variations but still the business fundamentals are similar. Your success will depend on your resiliency to adapt to the demands of the times. When starting your franchise business, it is imperative that the important aspects will be processed and not a single stone will be left unturned. The business registrations must be processed, proper taxes must be paid and corresponding registration of your trademarks and signs must be facilitated to protect the intellectual property rights of your business.

The franchisor must make sure that franchise operations manuals and franchise agreements are properly prepared. The legal and accounting aspects will play key roles when negotiating with prospective clients. Since a business is not only business but also a personal investment of owners in terms of time and money, it is important that all angles must be considered and that it must positioned to benefit not only the franchisor but more importantly, the franchisees. Nobody engages in business to lose money but to earn profit to support concurrent operations and to pay the payroll of employees.

Your business may experience headwinds during the course of its operations, which is normal in any business endeavor, and it is paramount that it must be commanded and controlled by experienced navigators who can travel the high seas using reserved arsenals to steer the business into safe harbors.

The winds of change will always be there, the sea of opportunities may be rough and the cyclones of competitions will deter your from achieving your goal of becoming a successful businessman but your firm resolve and unyielding guts will spell the big difference.

As Louis L'Amour, a best-selling American writer once said " Victory is won not in miles but in inches. Win a little now, hold your ground, and later, win a little more."

"If you don't build your dream, someone else will hire you to help them build theirs."

Dhirubhai Ambani, founder, Reliance Industries

CHAPTER 5

FRANCHISE SUCCESS FORMULA

Every businessman who wants to get a headway in the franchise industry knows the advantages of engaging the services of a Franchise Developer in developing their franchise program. Magn8 Ventures Inc. shares to you some tips and advantages of partnering with a Franchise Developer:

1) Designing and Upgrading of Franchise Operations Manual

A businessman may or may not have a set of operational manuals. In both cases, the expertise and background of a Franchise Developer in enhancing the Franchise Manuals will help a lot in promoting someone else's Franchise Business.

The operations manual embodies all the procedures needed from acceptance of franchisees up to the nitty gritty of things including store operations, personnel management and others. The enhancement of an existing franchise manuals will benefit your franchise business.

2) Mapping Out of Plans for Your Franchise Business

If the business is a battlefield, then the owners are the generals and the Franchise Developers are the advisors and intelligence officers. It is a must that before launching or converting your existing business into a franchise format, everything must be properly planned before it will be executed. For franchising, the improvement of operations and financial systems rest on the shoulders of the owners while the designing and development of the franchise manuals, franchise agreements, franchise marketing materials and the likes are the responsibilities of the

Franchise Developer. Both of them must work hand in hand in order for things to materialize as planned. It is a working partnership from beginning to the end.

3) Financial Systems Review

The most common slip-ups of most businessman is neglecting their accounting and tax systems. The common misnomer is that because one's business is not yet operational, they are not yet bound to file the proper forms with government agencies. Every tax must be properly filed, otherwise, the pain of paying penalties will affect the cash flow of your business. The need to establish an adequate accounting and tax system for the franchise business from the point of registration up to the operational stage is not to be ignored for it will have a material bearing on your business. The importance of having an accountant on your side is a necessity because they knew better the ins and outs of tax matters. All successful businesses in our country know this matter. If the big guys are doing it then the start-up companies must do it also.

4) Time, Motion and Money Advantages

If time is money, then every motion lost is money also. A businessman may be able to do all the manuals and everything for his franchise business but the professional inputs and experienced works of a Franchise Developer cannot be set aside and is irreplaceable in the long run. Every establish Franchising Brand in the market today, in one time of their operations, hired the services of a Franchise Developer in order to launch a more professional franchising program for their business. The time saved on getting the services of Franchise Developer will add value to your enterprise. The businessman knows the business entirety but the Franchise Developer dissects the important details that are often neglected that lead to the downfall of the business.

5) Two Heads Are Better Than One

That popular adage is almost always true in every situation in our life. The businessman may have the operational, sales and marketing knowledge but the franchising part is a blind and gray area for him. It takes two to tango. Just like in a dance, it is important that the other person not only knows how to dance but he knows how to dance well. Imagine the formula, established business plus a franchise developer equals a working franchise business. The benefits that your franchise business will reap will outweigh the cost of engaging the services of a franchise developer.

6) Always look at the positive side of life

This one thing in unquantifiable. Nobody can question the importance of this intangible in running the operations of your business. If you are going into business, you have to prepare for everything, the best and worst. If suddenly, you feel that everything is not going your way or it seems that everything is crumbling, you just have to look at the positive side of life. Setbacks and problems are only temporary. Smile and smell the flowers. Everything will be okay. Remember this popular saying, " He who has hope has everything".

7) You are in business not only for yourself but to make the world a better place to live

Sales and profit are important. That is beyond question. Imagine this. There are many businessmen today who wanted to generate revenue to fund their social causes. Some businesses allocate a portion of their profit or sometimes, majority of their profits to help the unemployed, the homeless, the persons with disabilities among others. They find satisfaction in helping them. If this aspect can be integrated in your business, it will have a tremendous multiplier effect.

"The more facts you tell, the more you sell. An advertisement's chance for success invariably increases as the number of pertinent merchandise facts included in the advertisement increases"

David Ogilvy, advertising tycoon

CHAPTER 6

LOCAL STORE MARKETING (LSM)

Once you launch your franchise business and you have already established a branch or store in a certain locality, what is the first thing that you have to do in order to promote your business?

It's local store marketing or LSM for short.

According to www.lsmguide.com, " local store marketing (also called neighborhood marketing) is marketing activities designed to help your business be locally relevant with your customers and community. Relevant in a way that helps you stay top of mind when they're considering your type of products and services". This type of marketing is geared to capture the purchasing decision of a given population within 1 to 5 kilometer radius from your store.

For example if the population of a given radius is 300,000, the most effective way to determine if your local marketing activities is effective is if you can attract 80-90% of that target market.
It may be quite challenging but there are some ways to do it.

It is the most effective way of reaching out to potential customers since you will go directly go to the targeted population. It may be tedious but certainly it will reach 100% of your intended -market. Before launching this kind of program, you have to conduct a cost-benefit analysis whether this kind of campaign will be effective in your area. You have to consider also the security risks when conducting this kind of campaign. Make an intelligent survey of the area first to make certain that your decision is right.

1) Distribution of Flyers and other promotional materials in key locations within your area

When you say key locations, we are referring to the most populous area within your city or municipality. It may be near the church, market, plaza, passenger terminals , subways, cluster of buildings and the likes. The more people on that particular area, the more effective your campaign will be. Nothing replaces thousands of warm bodies.

2) Using popular music and mascot during your store opening and during significant occasions

This kind of thing never loses it appeal. Mascot and popular music are two important things that always capture the hearts and minds of customers. You can use these two methods during your store opening, Valentine's Day, Christmas Day, town fiestas among others. The fiesta spirit is what people always love to see.

3) Conducting motorcade during store opening

You have to open your store with a big bang. Conducting motorcade during store opening and during important occasions can reach out to potential customers. You can bring your store mascot and let him wave to the crowd for marketing purposes. Make sure that you also bring banners, tarpaulins and others attractive marketing materials with you. The shirts that you will be wearing must colorful such as red, yellow and green.

4) Announcing your store opening at the local radio and cable stations

They also say that all politics are local, same with marketing. All marketing activities are also local. People love to engage with marketing people on the ground. Nothing replaces personal handshakes and personal touches.

Remember that customers always wanted a strong personal and deeper connection with a product or a brand.

5) Campus tours

When you say campus tour, you can conduct it in the elementary, high school and college level. The students comprise a major component of your customer base. You must not ignore this reality on the ground. Make sure also that you design a marketing campaign that will specifically cater to student customers like student meal, budget meal, school opening promo and the likes.

6) Sponsoring a local event or talent contest

As the popular saying goes, "when in Rome, do what the Romans do". In a simple parlance, you have to immerse in local activities especially their most important events. In the Philippines, they have this thing called fiesta where paper buntings or " banderitas" are sponsored by franchise companies to widen the scope of their marketing campaign. They also include the logos of their companies in tarpaulin materials to have a subliminal effects on the people who see these marketing materials.

7) Conducting a feeding program or scholarship program for local residents

During school openings, your store can sponsor feeding program for kids. This will help the school with their nutrition programs and at the same time it will elevate the level of consciousness of people about your products, services and brands. Sponsoring a local scholar will allow you company to be promoted as a socially responsible company and franchise brand.

These things may be simple but it will have a direct impact in your local store marketing program.

It is a wise and practical approaches to promote your franchise business and eventually increase your sales.

"I've only had two rules. Do all you can and do it

the best you can."

Colonel Sanders, KFC founder

CHAPTER 7

COMPLY WITH BUSINESS REGISTRATION REQUIREMENTS

Starting a business is the ultimate dream of almost everybody.

If you are an employee, you want to get out of the daily grind and you always aspire to gain financial freedom and acquire operational independence totally escaping the hustle and bustle of routinary and sometimes boring office works.

Aside from raising up the initial capital, do you know that the most important aspect that is often ignored by budding entrepreneurs and franchisors is the business registration, accounting and tax compliance angles?

That is why from the very start, you must make sure that these matters will be dealt with utmost care and attention.

If you miss the deadlines for filing and payments, it often results to fines and penalties. Such amount can be used to augment the financial and operational needs of your start-up business.

You are lucky if you are the accountant yourself. You can easily make schedules to comply with the government regulatory requirements. In the absence of this, make sure that you hire somebody who has an accounting, tax background and he or she has the know how of the inner workings of government compliances.

> "Whenever you see a successful business, someone once made a courageous decision."
>
> *Peter Drucker,Management consultant and educator*

CHAPTER 8

DRIVE THRU FEATURE WILL BE THE NEXT BIG THING

The drive-thru format is not actually a new concept.

According to Wikipedia," a drive-through or drive-thru (a sensational spelling of the word through), is a type of take out service provided by a business that allows customers to purchase products without leaving their cars. The format was pioneered in the United States in the 1930s by Jordan Martin, and has since spread to other countries."

Many companies, mostly franchise companies are integrating this concept to their store operations nowadays.

We can see this strategy being implemented by popular fast food companies, convenience store and gasoline stations.

Why is drive-thru a popular idea among business owners? Here are some of the advantages:

1) It's all about convenience

The very purposes of drive-thru concept is to target customers who are on the go, those who don't want to leave their cars and those who wanted food to be serve to them instantly.

How efficient and effective is this system?

According to the study made by QSR Magazine, " customers spend an average of 255 seconds in the drive-thru lane. Coming in just under 4.5 minutes." In the Philippines, it may vary but on the average it is a lot faster that falling in line inside the store.

2) It increases sales

Restaurants and other stores typically adopt the dine-in concept, the take-out concept and the online delivery concept. All these were adopted due to the effect of the COVID19 pandemic. By adding a drive-thru revenue stream, it becomes a strong hedging strategy for long-term business survival.

In a study made by www.QREAdvisors.com, they came out with the following facts:

· There is an estimated 200,000+ drive thru operations across the U.S. in 2020

· Americans visit drive-thru lanes about 6 billion times each year according to some statistics.

· 60% to 70% of most fast food sales come from drive-thru sales

· Drive-thru sales represent 70% of fast food sales which generates billions of dollars for the industry each month

· According to NPD Group, 57% of hamburger fast food customers use
the drive-thru lane, 40% with Mexican QSRs and 38% of chicken fast
food customers went straight to drive-thru lanes

· 34% of customers eat on-site at QSR Mexican restaurants with drive-
thru, while 26% prefer takeouts.

· Chicken chains have 25% dining in with 36% order to go

These are interesting facts that will become the basis to enhance your current marketing strategy.

That means to say, whenever one franchisor decides to open up a new store, he might consider adopting a drive-thru feature for it will add more sales and beef up their bottom lines.

As more and more people become more mobile and busier, they have lesser desire to go inside the restaurant and might as well proceed in the drive-thru lane.

As the proof of popularity of this concept, fast food restaurants are using not only one but usually two drive thru lanes.

One popular fast food store even said, " Two lanes are better than one."

"After World War II, I started my first company, Industrial Luncheon Service, with one truck and built it into a multistate fleet of 200 trucks and the largest food service business in New England. From there I opened a store called the Open Kettle in Quincy, Massachusetts, selling coffee and donuts. We renamed the store Dunkin' Donuts and the rest is history."

William Rosenberg

CHAPTER 9

FRANCHISE DEVELOPER WILL BE AN ACE IN YOUR SLEEVE

Every businessman who wants to get a headway in the franchise industry knows the advantages of engaging the services of a Franchise Developer.

As a practicing Franchise Developer, I want to share with you some tips and advantages of partnering with a Franchise Developer, why your store operations will become more professional once you engage their services.

1) Designing and Upgrading of Franchise Operations Manual

A businessman may or may not have a set of operational manuals. In both cases, the expertise and background of a Franchise Developer in enhancing the Franchise Manuals will help a lot in promoting someone else's Franchise Business. The operations manual embodies all the procedures needed from the acceptance of franchisees up to the nitty gritty of things including store operations, personnel management and others. The enhancement of an existing franchise manuals will benefit your franchise business.

2) Mapping Out of Plans for Your Franchise Business

If the business is a battlefield, then the owners are the generals and the Franchise Developers are the advisors and intelligence officers. It is a must that before launching or converting your existing business into a franchise format, everything must be properly planned before it will be executed. For franchising, the improvement of operations and financial systems rest on the shoulders of the owners while the designing and development of the franchise manuals, franchise agreements, franchise marketing materials and the likes are the responsibilities of the Franchise Developer. Both of them must work hand in hand in order for things to materialize as planned. It is a working partnership from beginning to the end.

3) Financial Systems Review

The most common slip-ups of most businessman is neglecting their accounting and tax systems. The common misnomer is that because one's business is not yet operational, they are not yet bound to file the proper forms with government agencies. The need to establish an adequate accounting and tax system for the franchise business from the point of registration up to the operational stage is not be ignored for it will have a material bearing on your business. The importance of having an accountant and a lawyer on your side is a necessity because they knew better the ins and outs of the business. All successful businesses in our country know this matter. If the big guys are doing it then the start-up companies must do it also.

4) Time, Motion and Money Advantages

If time is money, then every motion lost is money also. A businessman may be able to do all the manuals and everything for his franchise business but the professional inputs and experienced works of a Franchise Developer cannot be set aside and is irreplaceable in the long run. Every established Franchising Brand in the market today, in one time of their operations, hired the services of a Franchise Developer in order to launch a more professional franchising program for their business. The time saved on getting the services of Franchise Developer will add value to your enterprise.

The businessman knows the business entirety but the Franchise Developer dissects the important details that are often neglected that lead to the downfall of the business.

5) Two Heads Are Better Than One

That popular adage is almost always true in every situation in our life. The businessman may have the operational, sales and marketing knowledge but the franchising part is a blind area and even a gray area for him. It takes two to tango. Just like in a dance, it is important that the other person not only knows how to dance but he knows how to dance well. Imagine the formula, established business plus a franchise developer equals a working and a successful franchise business. The benefits that your franchise business will reap will outweigh the cost of engaging the services of a franchise developer.

Give the customers what they want, when and where they want it."

Joe C. Thompson Jr., 7-11 founder

CHAPTER 10

RIDING THE WINNING HORSE

Who will imagine that the business that will propel the world economy in greater heights in 2022 and probably beyond that will be the franchising business? The success of the franchise business became legendary since McDonald started doing it way back then. There are lots of businesses who became very successful when they took the franchising route. Imagine this, in the Philippines, milk tea and coffee business boomed during the pandemic. That was during the time when people are restricted to go out of their homes and were restricted to travel. That's how resilient franchise business is. Food is the numDber one product that is not affected even during inflationary period.

It is a common knowledge that the products that the franchisors are offering are not really new. These are ordinary products that are re-packaged and re-branded to make them attuned to the forces of change and the fast-paced business environment.

In the Philippines, they have launched these products for franchising:

- Coffee
- Milk Tea
- Pizzas
- Hamburgers
- Ricecakes
- French fries or potato fries
- Fishballs
- Dumplings
- Siomai
- Siopao
- Ice Scramble
- and almost all other food products
-

For non-food products, these are the most popular franchises:

- Laundry shops (they are so popular that you can see one shop per street corner)
- Beauty salon
- Gasoline stations
- Logistics and Courier companies
- Bookstore

- Car wash and car detailing
- and almost all other non-food products

Nothing new can be said about these products. So what makes them click to ordinary people?

BRANDING AND PACKAGING

The Filipinos being creative and entrepreneurial in nature had repackaged and repositioned common Filipino products and services into something professional and international in nature.

Filipino food franchise companies have the following common standard features:

POPULAR NAME, ATTRACTIVE, VERY VISIBLE AND WELL LIGHTED SIGNAGE.

A store or foodcart will not be complete without a unique and popular name (UNCLE JOHN, MANG KIKOS ISAWAN, MANG JUANS JUICE and others). Names are important for brand recall. The name of your brand must be retained in the memories of customers. A three syllable name can be easily recalled by clients. It should be colorful and well lighted, visible even from afar. Some store are also placing pylon signage aside from the store frontage signage for added visibility.

POPULAR AND PROFITABLE PRODUCTS

Any successful franchise owners will tell you that no matter how beautiful your store or foodcart is, it will not become profitable without a product or products that will sell in volume. After all, sales is the essence of business. Anchor products that can be easily sold should be displayed prominently in your stores or foodcarts.

CLEAN AND UNIFORMED CREW

The reason why the fastfood stores attracted number of clients is the clean, clean cut and uniformed crew. Nobody wants to buy products from a crew who dress shabbily, who hasn't taken his or her bath, who have long hair, unshaven face and most especially with crew who have long nails and unclean hands. Hygiene and sanitation always go side by side with saleable products.

PROFESSIONAL SALES AND ACCOUNTING PROCEDURES

There is a wide spread belief that since you only operate a very small store or you are selling only foodcart products, you don't have to devise an accounting system. That is entirely wrong. Business is business, no matter how small it is. The right and proper time to implement stringent accounting and sales procedures is when you are just starting. You solve a problem when they are just beginning to happen not afterwards. This is preventive measures. Corrective measures are very costly and time-consuming. or you can map out plans to join various events for the entire year.

BE A MEMBER OF DULY REGISTERED FRANCHISE ASSOCIATION

The franchise industry is a big, booming and multi billion dollar industry. Joining an industry association related to franchising will give a big boost to your franchise business. These associations are composed of businessmen who understand the ins and outs of franchising and can help you a lot in professionalizing your franchise business.

ATTEND AND JOIN TRADE FAIRS AND EXHIBITS

The easiest and the most cost effective way of promoting your franchise business is to join trade exhibits. During the exhibit, you can promote your products and services, you can introduce new business ideas, you can benchmark with your fellow businessmen and adapt their successful methods of doing business and even become part of SEMINARS during the exhibit proper. You can easily check the schedule of expos and exhibits online so that you can plan ahead of time

Something like 80 per cent of business decisions have a location element. In fact, it's probably higher than that.

Author: Jack Dangermond

CHAPTER 11

CRITERIA FOR GOOD AND IDEAL SITE OR LOCATION

Once you decided to go into franchising, either as franchisor or franchisee, it is very important that you will make a trade area survey of the possible location of your store. This is a very critical decision for your business because once you make a choice, you may encounter difficulties in transferring to another location if ever you change your mind later on due to contractual and cost considerations. It is imperative that you have to look for a location guided by the following parameters:

POPULATION

etermine the population of the place. The fastest way to do it is by finding the data in the internet. Most of the times, the population figure is mentioned there. If you want to determine the exact and the latest population figure, you can go the city hall or municipality where you are planning to establish your business and request for the data from the concerned person there.

Usually, for a franchise business, there is a ceiling that you have to meet in order to proceed in putting up store in that particular area. For example, some franchise companies set a limit of 100,000 people per 3 to 5 kilometer radius.

If the store is located on the ground floor of a building or condominium, the exact number of tenants living on that building or condominium is included in the algorithm plus the number of people living within the store trading area. Some franchise companies set a higher number of population to determine the demand for the services and products being offered by the franchise companies.

In a scientific manner, a trade area survey is conducted where the population and other demographics of the place is recorded in a trade area form.

It may be very technical for some but it is an approach that will be very helpful in making an informed decision in choosing the right location for your franchise business.

TRAFFIC GENERATORS

It is very important to note that traffic generators such as malls, drugstores, convenience stores, churches, government offices, schools among others have a very significant bearing in the success of your franchise business. People usually come in large numbers and converge on the mentioned locations for longer period of time which usually redound to your benefit. When people come, business usually flourish.

CAR AND PEDESTRIAN TRAFFIC

You have to determine if there are many people who will pass by your store every day. You can determine it by sitting in one particular restaurant near your place and stay there for one day. Make a count, use number counter and record it. For cars, you can also use a number counter. The most important thing in determining the car traffic is the speed of the car. Make sure the car is travelling in a slow mode. If the car is travelling at a speed of 60 kilometers or more per hour, that will be out of the equation. Usually, people riding on that car are busy people and they won't stop at your store to buy your products or avail of your services.

COMPETITION

Are there any other stores in your planned location offering products and services the same as yours. If yes, how many are offering the same products and services? It is important that you determine this matter so as not to divide the slice of the market. If you are the only one offering the product or service, that would definitely be a plus factor.

CHAPTER 12

RESEARCH AND DEVELOPMENT

As we all know, franchising is an evolving business. From a very simple franchise set-up a couple of years ago, today, it transformed itself into an exciting business concept. The advent of modern technology literary altered the business landscape that affected the ordering system, payment system, delivery system and logistical capabilities of each franchisor and franchisee.

Way back then, the most popular franchise concepts came from the United States and Canada. Today, we can see a lot of new faces emerging from the Southeast Asia and other parts of Europe. In the Philippines alone, there are more than 500 franchise brands that are being patronized by millions and millions of people. This franchise phenomenon will not stop and will continue to dominate the business industry in the next fifty years.

The internet makes it easier to franchise from the United

States and Canada to Southeast Asia and vice versa.

With that, franchisor and franchisee must continuously educate themselves with the latest trends in the market that they can adapt in their franchise business.

Here are some ways to keep yourself abreast of the latest development in the franchise industry.

Research and Development

Continuous research is one of the key to success of every business. Don't be contented with your existing operational systems as well as your current products you are offering to your clients. Look for an angle that will enhance the status of your business. The internet and other industry publications can help you in establishing a brand that will stand out in the market.

Harness fully the power of the internet

The internet is the most valuable information leveler. With the advent of new technology, every businessman is utilizing its power to the helm. With networking sites such as Linked in, Facebook, Instagram, Tiktok and Twitter, the ones using it to the maximum will be become the leader in the industry. Make a Facebook page for your own business in order to promote your products, new marketing strategies and photos of your business achievements. With million of internet users all over the world, the opportunities are limitless.

Also, don't forget to make a website for your franchise business, this will be an additional informational and marketing tool that should not be taken for granted.

FRANCHISING: WHAT WILL HAPPEN IN THE NEXT FIVE YEARS

Franchising is a very unique business concept for it involves lots of discipline ranging from marketing, finance, economics, arts and design among others.

Franchising is also a science which is defined by Oxford dictionary as " the intellectual and practical activity encompassing the systematic study of the structure and behavior of the physical and natural world through observation and experiment."

In the study made by www.statista.com, as of September 20, 2022, here are the significant facts:

- It is estimated that there will be some 792,000 franchise establishments in the United States
- The franchise industry in the United States is worth 827 billion dollars
- Franchise companies will employ 8.5 million people
- The largest segment of the franchising industry in the US is quick service restaurants (QSR) contributing over

276 billion dollars of the industry's total economic output
- The second largest segment of the franchising industry in the US is the business services accounting to around 100 billion dollars which includes real estate and commercial and residential services

How big is the franchising industry around the world?

If you are going to search google.com, you will find out this very interesting piece of information:

- Across the globe, one in seven businesses is a franchise- which equates to around 2,000,000 franchised companies, employing around 19,000,000 people

What is the state of franchising in the Philippines?

 ccording to the US International Trade Organization website published in 2020, here are interesting facts:

- The Philippines is a popular market for US franchises
- With a growing middle class, the Philippines is good market for franchises
- The market is extremely fond of American brands, where more than 90% of all foreign franchises are of U.S. origin

- Brands that have disappeared from the United States are still prominent in the Philippines, and nearly every mall hosts the same listing of standard American brands
- The Philippines is considered as one of the largest franchise markets in Southeast Asia
- Metro Manila alone, with a population of over 20 million during the day, is target market for foreign franchises
- The 4 million daily consumers dine and shop in the metropolis while visitors flock to stores that are in Manila to buy in bulk, and bring things back to their provinces
- Eating at a brand name establishment or purchasing brand name items signal societal status in one of the Asia's most social media savvy populations

I n the latest report of the Philippines Department of Trade and Industry (DTI), the country's trade secretary indicated that the Philippines is now the 7th largest franchise market in the world. He also enumerated the following significant market information:

- The country's retail and service franchises shared 7.8% to the GDP and created 2 million direct and indirect jobs

- Food makes up 43% of the estimated 1,800 franchise brands in the Philippines

- Citing food franchises have an aggregate value of P538 billion or $10.8 billlion

- The non-food service and retail subsectors each serve close to 1/3 of franchise brands in the country-service accounts for 29% of franchise brands in the Philippines and retail for 28%

For the next five years, from 2022-2027, we will see a lot of positive developments that will happen in the international and the Philippine franchise industry. The way I see it, the following will be the trend:

- Franchise companies will integrate technology in their store operations, use of digital kiosks to accept orders and process payments. Cashless transactions will play an important role in the day to day operations of these companies

- Use of drones in the delivery of products of franchise companies

- Flying cars will be used in the delivery of products of franchise companies. It may seem like a science fiction to some, however, come to think of it, many people did not believe scientist when they said that people will land on the moon. When that happened, people exclaimed, " it's unbelievable but it's a reality now"

- Online delivery will account to 80% of the sales of franchise companies. With technology at the helm of store operations, this thing will be a reality on the ground

- Almost all franchise companies will adopt the drive thru feature, with many people now have the financial capacity to own cars, it is a given that this concept will be integrated on the franchising plans of the management

- Customers will be able to order using their hologram image. They will not leave their own houses or offices, instead their virtual image will appear in front of the store counters and voila, they can now do instant ordering.

- Franchise companies from Asian countries like the Philippines will establish branches internationally. Meaning, their operations will not be confined on their own countries alone. We can see hundreds of branches of these Asian countries dominating the foreign business landscape. This one will be dubbed as, " The Golden Age of Asian Franchises"

These are some of my predictions and I think other good things will happen to the franchise industry that will make it even stronger and better than today.

A lot of notable franchise personalities will also give their testimonials that indeed the franchise industry is the industry that will be resilient and can strongly stand amidst the winds of changes that will happen throughout the world.

ABOUT THE AUTHOR

Vin Laurente is a Bachelor in Accountancy graduate of the Polytechnic University of the Philippines-Manila.

He has over 20 years combined experiences in the fields of accounting and finance, taxation, marketing, franchise development, website development, influencer marketing and website content management.